Edited by Gemma Curran | gemmacurran-digital.co.uk
Illustrations by Ashley Simpkins | ashleysimpkins.co.uk
Published by Jubilee Church Coventry | jubileechurchcoventry.org

FINDING BALANCE

in an unbalanced world

THANK YOU FOR TAKING TIME TO WORK THROUGH THIS BOOKLET.

You might simply want to get to know yourself better. Or you may have come here looking for help in a time of difficulty or stress. Either way, this booklet will show you a way of understanding how we function as human beings made in the image of God.

You'll find plenty of space in each chapter for jotting down ideas and thoughts as you reflect on what you're reading.

I have found, over several years of using this model, that it has helped many people to strengthen emotional health and develop resilience to withstand life's challenges. By increasing our understanding of ourselves – our emotions and our (often hidden) motivations – we can better understand our unwanted and confusing behaviours. We can learn how to work with our emotions, becoming empowered to make better decisions.

As a psychodynamic counsellor, I have drawn from decades of psychological research and practice by many experts. At the same time, I have held all this research and practice in the light of mainstream biblical teaching. These two foundations of my work have been condensed into the accessible model laid out in this booklet.

Each chapter introduces you to ideas that expand your understanding of how you function. Stories in the chapters give you examples of how this plays out in real life. I have also included exercises to help you apply these ideas to your life.

Take your time working through each section of the booklet. As you do so, you will find some parts resonating with you more strongly than others. Take extra time over the things that stand out; reflect on them.

God is in the business of transforming each one of us *"from one degree of glory to another"* (2 Corinthians 3:18 ESV). My hope and prayer is that he will use this booklet as his tool to do just that for you.

Steve Atkinson, November 2024

A RATIONAL, EMOTIONAL GOD

God is both a rational and an emotional being.

How is God rational?

When we focus on God's creation, his supreme logic and amazing rationality are manifestly apparent; there is a logical, rational, ordered mind behind it.

Life in all its forms is made up of billions and billions of atoms, all interlinked and interconnected.

Humans have spent centuries, if not millennia, trying to understand the mysteries of his creation, including his creation of humans themselves. We have invested time and energy into this for hundreds of years. The Hadron Collider took 20 years to plan, 10 years to build, cost 3.7 billion dollars and costs much, much more to run. All in the pursuit of discovering the fundamental particles that make up everything.

Consider the atom. There are only a few types of atom that make up everything, from diamonds to soil to people. We are made up of trillions of these atoms and they come together in very specific and specialised ways to make up all the components of a human being.

For you to exist, countless numbers of atoms must interact and organise in a way that is unique to you. In fact, because you are unique, this is the only time those atoms are going to combine in that way. It will never happen again.

Atoms do not think, and they are not even alive, unlike you. If those atoms that make up the physical you were to detach themselves from each other, we would be left with just a pile of dust. "Dust to dust" as the common paraphrase of Genesis 3 puts it. God devised this mechanism!

That is only a partial glimpse into one small part of his creation. My wife remembers the eureka moment when, as a child in a classroom studying biology, she heard for the first time that plants absorb carbon dioxide and convert it into oxygen. Conversely, humans need oxygen to breathe and live, giving out carbon dioxide which is poisonous to them. Two different parts of God's creation, designed to be interdependent, supply each other's needs.

Her immediate thought was how clever God was. Clever and rational.

God not only created us human beings, deeply complex as we are, but he also created the stars, the plants, the animals, the air that we breathe. He thought them up, he devised them, he conceived them. They are all interrelated. It is incredible isn't it?

In fact, logic forms the foundation on which maths, physics, biology, chemistry and every discipline of science is built – and determines the interactions between each one.

God devised it all. What an intelligent, creative, rational mind!

Rational in at least two senses.

He is objective. In fact, he is the essence of objectivity: his word is objectively true. His word is the measure and arbiter of all truth.

He is logical. He provides the solution to any problem. The problem of sin (and the consequent separation of man from him) is perhaps the ultimate example. His solution? The incarnation and death on the cross of God himself.

God is rational.

How is God emotional?

God is also emotional. Just a quick scan of the Bible and you'll see it.

- He gets angry: *"The Lord's anger burned against Moses."* (Exodus 4:14)

- He avenges: *"The Lord is a God who avenges"* (Psalm 94:1); *"It is mine to avenge; I will repay."* (Deuteronomy 32:35)

- He gets distressed: *"In all their distress he too was distressed."* (Isaiah 63:9)

- He cares and loves: *"The Lord set his affection on your ancestors and loved them, and he chose you, their descendants, above all the nations – as it is today."* (Deuteronomy 10:15)

- He shows concern: *"I have indeed seen the misery of my people… and I am concerned about their suffering."* (Exodus 3:7)

- He can be jealous: *"The Lord is a jealous…God."* (Nahum 1:2)

- He is compassionate: *"As a father has compassion on his children, so the Lord has compassion on those who fear him."* (Psalm 103:13)

- He experiences joy and he delights: *"He will take great delight in you… he will rejoice over you with singing."* (Zephaniah 3:17)

Notice that these are all Old Testament examples – and just a handful at that. It's not just Jesus, fully God and fully man, who is emotional. The LORD is emotional, Father, Son and Holy Spirit.

So, when Jesus says, *"Anyone who has seen me has seen the Father"* (John 14:9) and Paul writes that *"the Son is the image of the invisible God"* (Colossians 1:15), we know that Jesus the Son is reflecting the character of the Father – emotions and all.

What about us?

In Genesis 1:26-27 we read God saying, *"'Let us make mankind in our image, in our likeness.' ... So God created mankind in his own image, in the image of God he created them; male and female he created them."* Therefore, we are made in God's image. Just as God is rational and emotional, we are rational and emotional. We conceptualise, we reason, we apply logic, we analyse, we find solutions; we are rational. We get angry, we experience sorrow, we care, we get jealous, we feel joy; we are emotional.

It is helpful to think of ourselves as having a rational side and an emotional side. We can define rational as the ability to think through problems, weigh up the pros and cons, find solutions and make conscious decisions.

Our rational side is aware of the consequences of our actions, it exercises control, it stops us doing something that is foolish or dangerous. It is objective, allowing us to stand back, observe ourselves and think things through.

Emotions are involved in making attachments – in forming and maintaining relationships. Without them, family, friendships and church community would mean very little.

Additionally, our feelings warn us of possible threat. They assess our environment 'instinctively': is it safe, is it good? Is it bad, scary or dangerous? Recent neuroscientific research has found that the part of our brain that processes emotions picks up these signals faster than the part that deals with rational thought.

And of course, our God-given conscience uses emotions to help us do what is morally right.

Our emotional side is God-given, just as our rational side is.

But we are a fallen people in a fallen world and our rational and emotional sides operate in a fallen way.

The emotional side of us is wild. It is not tame. It feels what it feels, it is not logical, not rational, it just is. It is raw and it feels like it comes from a long way down. It can take us by surprise. It can be confusing, it can be scary, it can be passionate and powerful. It can be overwhelming.

And our rational side can ignore the emotional side of us, dismiss our feelings and drive us regardless of the emotional consequences. It doesn't consider how something impacts not just our well-being, but also our relationships. It can ignore the spiritual side of life, limiting our relationship with God and our joy in his creation to what can be rationally experienced.

We are wired up to be rational and emotional. And both these parts of us are fallen, corrupted by a fallen world. We are fallen people in a fallen world.

WRITE IT OUT...

When do I tend to be rational?

When do I tend to be emotional?

BALANCE

Like our creator we are rational and emotional beings.

Neither our rational side nor our emotional side is wrong or more important than the other: they are designed to be held in balance.

However, various pressures on us as we grow up, or through society, can influence the way we feel about them.

For example, if we are brought up in a family where being rational is emphasised and emotions are not talked about, we can end up believing that emotions are embarrassing, annoying, unimportant, self-indulgent, or downright wrong. So we are encouraged to ignore them and focus on logic instead.

Alternatively, if we are surrounded by adults who act out their emotions, being volatile, angry, very sad, happy or excited in an uncontrolled way, we can find ourselves becoming very emotional people. We are taught 'if it feels right, then it is right', so we surrender ourselves to our emotions, ignoring the consequences.

God may have created us in his image, with both a rational and an emotional side – but our society and background might emphasise one over the other, leading to an unhealthy imbalance.

John's parents had been brought up in violent households. Because of this they did not like voices to be raised in the family home. Whenever John or any of his siblings got cross, or even passionate about something, they would be told to soften their voices or be sent to their bedrooms.

In John's adult relationships this became problematic. Whenever his girlfriend was upset about something and was trying to express it, John would instinctively react by trying to quieten her down. His girlfriend experienced this as John shutting her down and him not accepting her feelings.

WRITE IT OUT...

Using John's story as a starting point, think about examples of societal or family pressures or expectations to:

suppress emotions

suppress thinking things through rationally

Our goal is to develop balance. The two sides of us are complimentary; this is the way we are created – to be rational and emotional beings just like our creator God.

WRITE IT OUT...

I have come across people over the years who are out of balance. They have either ignored or suppressed their emotional side, or they have ignored their rational side and just gone with their emotions. All of us are on that spectrum somewhere.

Take time to consider. Where do you think you are on the spectrum between rational and emotional? Mark your place and make some notes about why you think you're there.

RATIONAL   EMOTIONAL

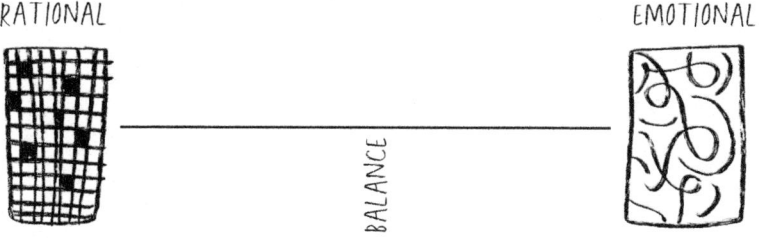

BALANCE

THE COST OF IMBALANCE

So many of the problems we face in life come when we ignore one side or the other, becoming imbalanced.

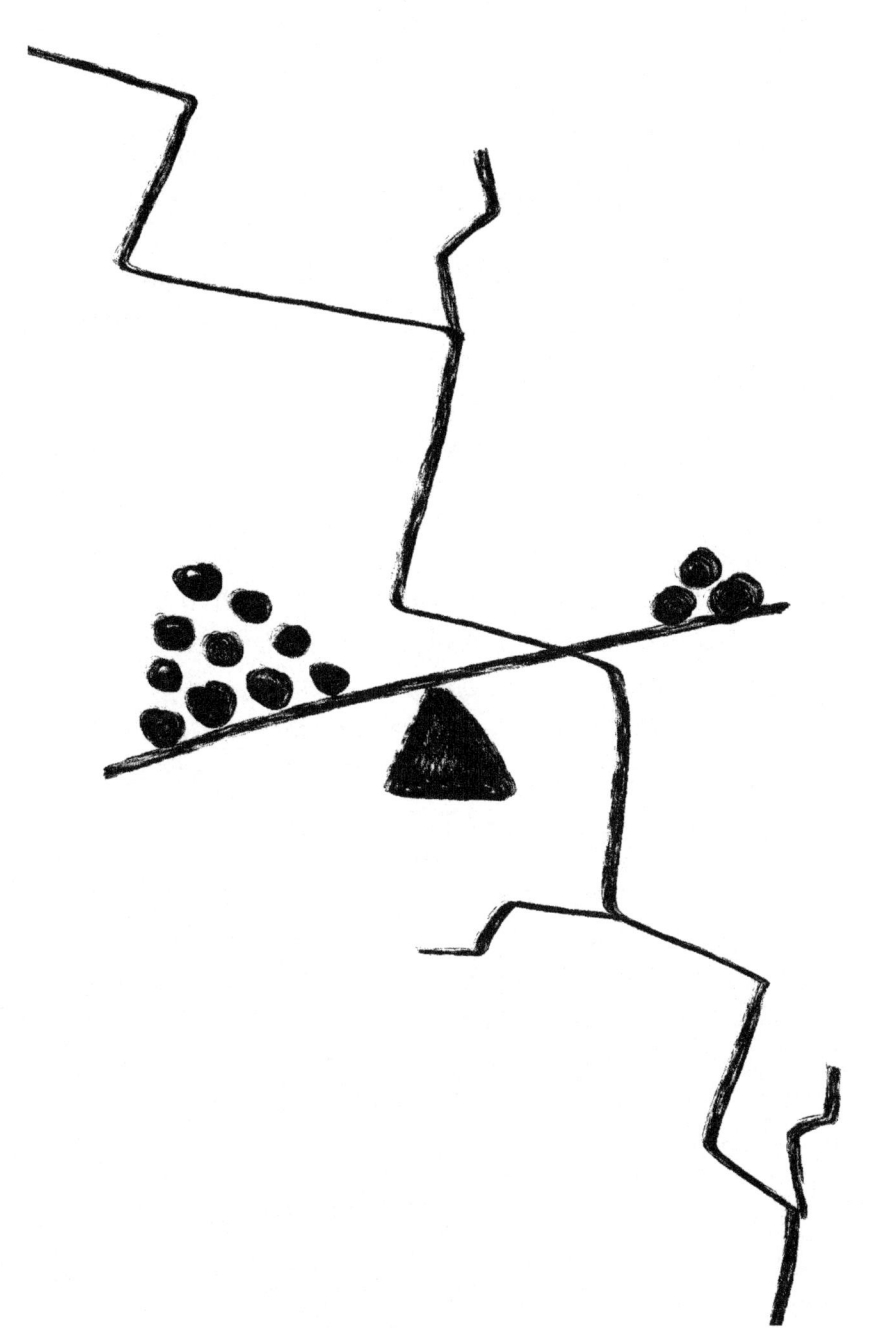

Ignoring our emotional side

Ignoring your emotions does not make them go away.

In fact, it is like putting them in a pressure cooker and fastening down the lid. What happens? There will eventually be an explosion.

When I worked in a drug rehabilitation centre we had a saying: if you suppress your emotions, they will 'come out sideways'. Emotions do not go away, and they have to come out somewhere. So, if ignored, they can explode out (or seep out) at a time when you may not expect it and be directed at someone or something that does not deserve it. Here is an example:

I have had a bad day at work. I had spent days preparing a presentation and at the last minute my boss had cancelled it and told the team that something else was prioritised. What made it worse was that he had been quite dismissive of me in front of colleagues. I did not feel confident enough to tackle him about it, so I go home at the end of the day feeling disillusioned with the whole job situation and undermined by my boss.

When I get home, I snap at my wife over something minor and go out for a walk to get some air. My wife, now feeling out of sorts, ends up shouting at the kids when she sees how untidy their bedroom is. One of the kids kicks the dog and the dog is left thinking "what have I done?" The anger that belonged to me and should have been directed towards my boss ends up directed at the dog.

This is a comic example of emotions 'coming out sideways'. Suppressing bigger, more important emotions brings bigger, more important consequences - exploding out sideways some way down the line.

The impact isn't just relational; it can also have physical consequences. Suppressing important and powerful emotions over weeks, months or years can lead to breakdowns or physical illness. Poor emotional health can cause poor physical health.

Do you ever find yourself behaving in a way that puzzles you? Or in a row with a partner or friend and wonder how you got there?

Do you wonder why you worry when you do not need to or why you say something hurtful in the heat of the moment?

Do you ever wonder why you cannot stop eating even if you really want to stop?

Do you puzzle over why you keep repeating the same mistakes in relationships?

These are all examples of the emotional side of you at work, whether you like it or not! Emotions do not go away. They have to be processed.

Shaun began suffering from back pain for no apparent reason. He was in an intense, physically demanding job, so thought that was why. He saw doctors, went to physio and went running to try and alleviate his symptoms. While he got to the point of managing the pain, it didn't go away.

Years later, he read a book about anger and its physical impacts. He realised that he'd been suppressing anger for a long time. Amazingly, as he dealt with his pent-up anger, his back pain subsided until it disappeared. He hasn't had back problems since.

WRITE IT OUT...

Think of a time when you tried to pretend that you did not feel the way you were feeling. Write it down, reflect on it. How did that work out for you? Did it go away never to come back again?

Ignoring our rational side

We have considered the danger of ignoring our emotional side. What happens if we ignore our rational side?

Emotions are wild and volatile; they can change day by day, sometimes hour by hour. They are influenced by our physical state, by lack of sleep, by bad diet, by hormones, even by the weather!

So, if we ignore our rational side and rely on our emotional side, we open ourselves up to being blown this way and that by them. We can be overwhelmed, confused, and make bad decisions which we later regret.

From before he was married, Tom has found that being good at his job has made him feel good about himself.

Since getting married and having children he has become aware that he's been using work as an escape. Whenever he and his wife have a disagreement, when there is tension between them, or an issue with the children, he purposely works longer hours – sometimes sacrificing weekend family time.

Deep down, he knows that when he does this, he is just temporarily avoiding the problems at home. The short-term good feelings produced by his work actually undermine his marriage and negatively affect the family.

Nevertheless, he regularly reverts to this behaviour to give himself temporary relief.

WRITE IT OUT...

Can you think of a time when you were led by your emotions or let them take over? What were the repercussions for you? What were the repercussions for others?

What do you feel about that now?

THE BENEFITS OF BALANCE

It's clear that ignoring either our emotional or rational sides has significant consequences for our whole lives. The solution is all about balance.

To function in a healthy way, we need to have our rational side and our emotional side in balance. Neither one suppressed; neither one dominant.

An illustration:

> *I come into the house and tell my housemate that the man next door had blocked our car in by parking across the driveway and I had to tell him to move it. My housemate responds by saying "I don't know why you're making such a big deal of it – it got sorted didn't it?"*

The rational side of me thinks *"I wasn't really making a big deal of it but clearly my housemate doesn't want to hear, so I'll just let it go."* Or, *"It did get sorted so she has probably got a point and I need to move on and not react."*

The rational part of me recognises my housemate's logic and pushes it to one side. It continues to bother me all evening and I go to bed feeling tense and stressed.

The emotional side of me, however, has a different response. It takes the remark personally and responds emotionally.

I find myself saying *"Why don't you ever support me?"* Or *"I'm not making a big deal out of it – what's your problem?"* Or *"I only made a comment that I thought you, as my friend, might be interested in!"* You can imagine how the conversation could go downhill from there!

In the first responses I am being led by my rational side, in the second by my emotional side. We must strike a balance. We cannot ignore or suppress our rational side or our emotional side. Doing either of those things is not healthy and it is not the way God has made us to be.

WRITE IT OUT...

Think about a time when you found yourself asking 'how did I get into this situation?'

Was it a repeating pattern?

Do you think it was because you suppressed emotions or because emotions were in control?

The power of the internal dialogue

We achieve balance by having a dialogue between our rational side and our emotional side. An internal conversation.

Suppressing our emotions does not help, so first of all we must acknowledge them. Rationally, objectively, we can say to ourselves 'I am feeling like this…' We stop, reflect, acknowledge how we are feeling and actually voice it – internally or some other way.

This starts the process of releasing emotional pressure from the 'pressure cooker'. The emotional part of us must be heard, must be acknowledged by us. It must be validated. It is a very powerful drive within us; our feelings want to be taken seriously. It is how we are wired up.

How do we do this practically? How do we acknowledge and validate our feelings?

We do this by beginning an internal conversation between the two parts of us – both our rational and emotional sides. The conversation starts like this:

"I am feeling like this…"	Acknowledge your feelings and emotions
"I wonder why I feel like this? What has been going on that makes me feel like this?"	Exploring their source
"No wonder I feel like this!"	Validating your emotions

How might this apply to me telling my housemate about the neighbour who parked his car across our drive? At some point during, or after, our conversation (or row!) I could have had that dialogue between my rational and emotional side:

"I am feeling like this..." Acknowledge your feelings and emotions	*"I am feeling defensive and touchy."*
"I wonder why I feel like this? What has been going on that makes me feel like this?" Exploring their source	*"Well, I did have a rubbish day at work where my boss undermined me. And I know that I really do not like confrontation. So, it was really hard for me to ask the neighbour to move his car."*
"No wonder I feel like this!" Validating your emotions	*"No wonder I am feeling defensive and touchy. It all makes sense now."*

The results of this conscious internal dialogue are fascinating. Once you have brought your feelings and their source into awareness, you take the power out of them.

You are no longer pushed around by them in a mystifying way. You can then move on to making a decision about what you do about it, adding an extra step:

"I am feeling like this..."	Acknowledge your feelings and emotions
"I wonder why I feel like this? What has been going on that makes me feel like this?"	Exploring their source
"No wonder I feel like this!"	Validating your emotions
"In the past when I felt like this, I ended up doing x, y or z. But actually, I do not have to do it, do I?"	Consciously deciding how to respond or act

Using your rational side, you come to understand and validate your emotional side. You become aware of what is going on for you, taking the power out of your emotions. You can then make a conscious decision, a rational decision, about how you are going to respond to the situation.

In the example I gave of me, my housemate and my neighbour's car, I could remember that at times like this I often get into an argument. Instead, I could choose to de-escalate it and talk about what's really been difficult in my day.

"You're right, it's not a big deal that I had to speak to the neighbour about the car. I think I'm feeling a bit defensive and touchy actually, it was a difficult day..."

Imagine what a different kind of conversation I could have had with my housemate now!

WRITE IT OUT...

Take the situation you wrote down in the last exercise. Use the table below to work through that moment and consider what achieving balance might look like.

"I am feeling like this..." Acknowledge your feelings and emotions	
"I wonder why I feel like this? What has been going on that makes me feel like this?" Exploring their source	

*"No wonder I feel
like this!"*
Validating your
emotions

*"In the past when I
felt like this, I ended
up doing x, y or z.
But actually, I do not
have to do it, do I?"*
Consciously deciding
how to respond or act

BUILDING RATIONAL AND EMOTIONAL BALANCE

By becoming both rationally and emotionally aware, we are able to find balance.

Becoming aware of our emotions

Not all of us find accessing our emotions easy.

But to achieve balance, we need to become emotionally aware. We need to be able to complete the sentence, "I am feeling…"

Emotional awareness is a skill that can be developed. If you are someone who thinks you never know what you are feeling, you can work on it and get better at it.

First of all, we all need to slow down and give ourselves time and space. We need to give ourselves the opportunity to reflect. To think. To ask ourselves 'how am I feeling?' If we do not stop and ask, we will not get an answer.

Your feelings, your emotions, are there and affecting you, even if you are not consciously aware of them. You need to give yourself time and space to access them.

Being busy all the time is a way of suppressing your feelings. Workaholics are not healthy people! A key to being emotionally healthy is to give yourself regular time when you can just stop and think. Think about how you feel and have that internal dialogue.

When we have slowed down and made space, we might still find it difficult to get in touch with our emotions and for some of us it can be baffling. Here are some things you can try[1]:

- Keep a private notebook to record things that have been going on for you. When you have reflective time, write down what has been happening and what you think about it. Then move on from what you think about it to what you feel.

- Do something artistic. Art is a way of expressing emotion non-verbally. Music, art, movement or poetry are all helpful.

1 There are lots of different ideas in the Healthy Habits chapter at the end of the book.

Maria makes sure that she schedules in a couple of hours every week to go for a walk and reflect on how her week is going. She gives herself time to consider how events at work or at home are impacting her. When she has this time, she feels better able to deal with the challenges of the week.

When she doesn't get this time, she feels less stable, less sure of herself and less able to cope with the unexpected. It makes a real difference to her and those around her.

WRITE IT OUT...

Think through your week and decide on just 10 minutes to spend considering your emotions. Choose a time when you often feel calm and will be uninterrupted. Choose a place where you will feel safe.

I am going to spend ten minutes thinking about my emotions on _____(d a y) at _____(time).

To help me process my emotions, I am going to...

(Stuck for ideas on how to get started? Check out the Healthy Habits chapter at the end of this book for inspiration.)

Becoming rationally aware

It is helpful to think of two sorts of rational. There is 'common sense' rational and there is 'rational faith'.

Common sense rational

It is common sense to expect an emotional reaction to significant events in your life.

Maybe you recently lost your job. You would rationally expect to feel low after that. So, you would be able to reflect and in that internal dialogue say to yourself "no wonder I am feeling down, it is not a surprise, I lost my job last week."

That is 'common sense' rational.

Perhaps you feel tearful, and your mood might be swinging up and down. On reflection, you know that it is 'that time of the month' – the mood swings are not surprising.

All sorts of things affect us: life events, lack of sleep, work problems, bad diet, hormones, what is going on for our loved ones, not being able to see our loved ones, big changes happening in our life…

We can rationally understand our emotional reactions and make allowances for ourselves. That is common sense rationality.

John was having a bit of a low time but for a while he tried to ignore it and 'just get on with it'.

Finally, he decided to treat himself and go fishing – something that always helped him to feel grounded.

While he contemplated the flowing water it occurred to him that it was coming up to the anniversary of his mother's death. The penny dropped as he realised the source of his low mood. Although the sadness didn't just disappear, now he understood the cause of his low mood, it all felt more manageable. He resolved to be kind to himself in the coming weeks.

WRITE IT OUT...

Write a list of the most stressful life events you've experienced. If you can, note down some emotions you would expect from these events.

Rational faith

The second kind of rational is rational faith. This is not a new concept: it is what Christians have been doing since the year zero (literally).

Rational faith is about logically, objectively, reasonably and analytically applying God's Word to our lives. We can then use it in the dialogue between our emotional side and our rational side. Our rational faith converses with our emotions so that we can apply God's truth to our situation.

Feelings are subjective; even 'common sense' can be twisted or distorted. But God's truth is the truth. We can use it as we dialogue with our emotional side.

"I don't feel loved"

Let's say you don't feel loved, or even feel unlovable. What does rational faith say?

The truth is that God loves you so much that he sent his Son to die for you. That is the biblical truth.

> "For God so loved the world that he gave his one and only Son, that whoever believes in him shall not perish but have eternal life." (John 3:16)

> "God demonstrates his own love for us in this: While we were still

sinners, Christ died for us." (Romans 5:8)

"*I feel abandoned*"

In another example, you might be feeling abandoned, that no-one is interested in you or your welfare.

The truth is that God knows you better than you know yourself. He knew you in your mother's womb and he knows you now. He sees everything that happens to you, and he will never let you go.

> "*Where can I go from your spirit? Where can I flee from your presence? If I go up to the heavens, you are there;*
>
> *if I make my bed in the depths, you are there. If I rise on the wings of the dawn,*
>
> *if I settle on the far side of the sea, even there your hand will guide me, your right hand will hold me fast.*
>
> *If I say, "Surely the darkness will hide me and the light become night around me," even the darkness will not be dark to you; the night will shine like the day,*
>
> *for darkness is as light to you. For you created my inmost being;*
>
> *You knit me together in my mother's womb.*" (Psalm 139)

Do you see how you can apply the truth of the bible to your situation and balance it against your emotions?

Susan began suffering from anxiety and insomnia during the Covid lockdown. She would have panic attacks in the middle of the night, sometimes lasting for hours. This had a huge impact on her physical health as well as her mental health.

However, God gave Susan a verse to contemplate during those long hours of being awake or while experiencing a panic attack: "Do not fear, for I am with you. Do not be dismayed, for I am your God. I will strengthen you and help you; I will uphold you with my righteous right hand." (Isaiah 41:10).

Whenever Susan was afraid, unable to sleep, or panicking, she would recite these words to herself. Her anxiety didn't disappear straight away, but she began to trust God in the midst of it; his word gave her faith. Over time, the panic attacks stopped. The anxiety disappeared, and Susan could sleep again. And Susan has a greater ability to trust God, whatever she faces.

WRITE IT OUT...

Have a go with the following statements. Find bible verses that can help us with the feelings below by applying God's truth:

"I feel afraid."

"I feel sad."

"I feel _____."

There are no negative emotions

There is a temptation to suppress what some identify as negative emotions.

Anger is a good example. We might be feeling angry and in our dialogue between our emotional side and our rational faith, we might use Ephesians 4:26 which tells us, *"In your anger do not sin."* So, we can use that to stop us acting on our anger and doing something unwise or wrong.

But notice that scripture does not say 'do not get angry', it says *"in your anger do not sin."* This is a really important point, and one that can get us into a tangle if we misunderstand it.

It is an easy trap to fall into. The lie is that it is wrong to have emotions like anger, sadness, anxiety, fear: feelings that are widely considered 'negative emotions'.

We can begin to think that the Bible says feeling those emotions means there is something wrong with us. That we do not have enough faith or are not good enough Christians.

This is not true. And this kind of thinking, whether we are aware of it or not, causes us to suppress our emotions. This is both emotionally and physically unhealthy.

I prefer to describe these emotions as 'uncomfortable emotions'.

The Bible is full of great men and women of God feeling uncomfortable emotions and expressing them to God. Amazingly, God meets them in the midst of their emotions and has a positive relationship with them.

We don't try to avoid uncomfortable emotions. We simply do not let them dominate us. We get them into balance with the rational – and with rational faith. We acknowledge and validate our emotions, and then apply God's truth to the way we are feeling.

Let's see the shape of our internal dialogue when we add rational faith in:

"I am feeling like this…"	Acknowledge your feelings and emotions
"I wonder why I feel like this? What has been going on that makes me feel like this?"	Exploring their source
"No wonder I feel like this!"	Validating your emotions
"In the past when I felt like this, I ended up doing x, y or z. But actually, I do not have to do it, do I?"	Consciously deciding how to respond or act
"I can try to trust in God's word – in fact I can ask him to help me do that – I will hang on and have faith in him."	Turning to God for the truth to provide balance to my emotions, give me a sense of perspective and help me to handle them

WRITE IT OUT...

Read through Psalm 55. Can you see the psalmist's journey through their internal dialogue to rational faith? Track it in the table below.

"I am feeling like this..." What are the psalmist's emotions?	
"I wonder why I feel like this? What has been going on that makes me feel like this?" Why does the psalmist feel that way?	
"No wonder I feel like this!" How does the psalmist validate his emotions?	

"In the past when I felt like this, I ended up doing x, y or z. But actually, I do not have to do it, do I?"
How does the psalmist respond to his emotions?

"I can try to trust in God's word – in fact I can ask him to help me do that – I will hang on and have faith in him."
How does the psalmist apply his knowledge of God - his rational faith - to his situation and what he's feeling?

CAPACITY AND RESILIENCE

In the final section of this booklet, I am going to look at an important practicality: capacity.

It might come as a shock to some of us (especially if we are under twenty-five years of age), but we all have limited capacity. God has unlimited capacity, but we do not.

My loose definition of capacity is about quantity. It is about how much you can carry.

Someone who is holding down three jobs, caring for a sick parent, paying two mortgages, home educating their children, volunteering at a homeless centre, and leading a church, has a huge capacity. They also do not exist!

We all have limited capacity. Everyone has different levels of capacity, and those levels change over time, often dependent on life-stages.

It is useful to think of your capacity as being like an inner battery: when it is fully charged up you can do all sorts of things and cope with the demands that are made of you. But if your 'capacity battery' is nearly empty even the smallest new demand seems like too much to bear.

There are things that charge up your battery, and things that deplete it. There are people who charge up your battery, and others who deplete it.[1]

---

1   Putting people on your deplete list does not mean they are bad people or that there is something wrong with them. It is about how your personality functions and how theirs does. Someone who might deplete you may well charge someone else up. You don't have to avoid them, but when your capacity battery is low and you need it charging up, you will need to take it into consideration.

Lucy has a friend who has physical and mental health problems, and a challenging family life. Her friend, Clare, was quite isolated and often struggled to manage everything that was happening. Lucy did her best to make herself available whenever she was needed. To do the Christian thing and help someone in need!

However, Lucy slowly realised that this wasn't healthy. She was answering calls and messages in the middle of her working day, or while making dinner, or while playing with her children. She found it quite draining making time for Clare, especially when Clare was in a bad place. It was having an impact on her capacity to give attention to her children and her emotional energy for her husband.

Lucy realised that she needed to put some healthy boundaries around the time she spent with Clare. So, every time the phone rang or a message came through, she would stop and pray. "Should I pick up the phone, God?" Taking a moment to pause and think meant Lucy could make herself available when she had the capacity to do so but could also not be available when she needed to focus on something else. She's been able to continue supporting Clare without it negatively impacting on her or her family.

Lucy was surprised to find that the time she does spend with Clare has become less draining, simply because she knows she has a boundary in place.

WRITE IT OUT...

Draw up two lists. Make the first a list of things that charge you up; the second a list of things that deplete you. Include people!

What charges me up?	What depletes me?

Maintaining capacity

It is a good idea to keep lists of those things and people that charge up your capacity battery and those that deplete you. When your capacity feels low, you can do some activities that charge you up or cut back on some of those things that deplete you.

Remember that everyone is different. What might deplete you might charge someone else up - and your capacity can fluctuate at different times.

It is very important to be aware of your capacity and to keep monitoring it.

Firstly, because you need to manage it and make decisions about what new things you can take on.

Secondly, because your capacity affects your resilience.

Remaining resilient

Resilience refers to your ability to cope with stress.

If you are resilient, when a shock or a setback comes along - an illness or a hardship – you are more able to easily come back from it, to regain equilibrium. You are more able to recover quickly. But the opposite is true if you are not resilient when the setback comes.

Capacity deeply affects resilience. If you are stretched to the maximum and a setback comes along, your resilience is going to be low and you may struggle to recover. It will certainly take longer to reach an equilibrium.

So keep an eye on your capacity levels. If you do suffer a setback or a hardship and you are having trouble recovering, review your commitments. Pay attention to the things that charge your battery up and make sure that you put them in place.

Even better, employ preventative measures. Don't let your capacity get down into the red. Keep something in reserve. Be self-aware. This is self-care, not only for your benefit but also for those whom you love and care for.

Sue had been working extra hours for the last two weeks so that she could meet a deadline at work. This had been difficult as her elderly mother was recovering in hospital after a fall. Sue was worried about her and had started the process of getting some help for her from social services; a complex and confusing process.

One night, after she had got home late after visiting her mother in hospital, she got a phone call from a church member saying that she was no longer going to be able to be on the children's work rota that Sue organised. Normally she would have taken this in her stride, but she did not have the headspace to work out what to do about it. When she woke up the next morning, even though it was the first thing that came into her mind, she put off thinking about a solution.

Half an hour before she was due to leave for work her daughter phoned. She had argued with her fiancé and they had parted on bad terms. She did not know if the relationship was over and wanted Sue's advice and sympathy.

Sue felt totally overwhelmed and very upset; it was 'the straw that broke the camel's back.' She felt like she did not have anything left to give and this piece of news from her daughter felt disproportionately disastrous. She did not know how she was going to cope with what today was going to bring – work, her visit to her mother, finishing and submitting the social services form and having to sort out the rota - let alone finding the inner resources to comfort and advise her daughter.

WRITE IT OUT...

List the things that impacted Sue's resilience from the story above. If Sue had been aware of her low capacity at the beginning of the story, what might she have done differently?

Where is your capacity at the moment? Draw a level on the battery.

EMPTY

FULL

Why did you choose that level for your battery?

Can you think of a time when you weren't very resilient to a shock or setback? Perhaps something had a disproportionate impact on you or caused you to 'crash out' in an unexpected way. What happened before that to reduce your resilience?

SUMMARY

Here's a summary of everything we've explored in this booklet:

- We are rational and emotional beings, made in God's image

- It is healthy to have our rational and emotional sides in balance

- We achieve balance by having dialogue between our rational side and our emotional side

- There are two sorts of rational – 'common sense rational' and 'rational faith'

- It is helpful to work on our emotional awareness

- It is important to pay attention to our capacity battery

- Good capacity management gives us resilience

All that remains is to put what we have learned into practice. Easier said than done!

Just remember that it takes time and effort to build up your emotional health and resilience. Be intentional about working on it, particularly your self-awareness. And remember – be kind to yourself and be patient.

Invite God to change the areas that need some work. Our loving, kind and patient God is in the business of changing us *"from one degree of glory to another"* (2 Corinthians 3:18).

WRITE IT OUT...

In what area(s) do you need to invite God to help you? Where is God inviting you to change? Use these two pages to make some notes for yourself.

HEALTHY HABITS

There are no right or wrong ways of creating time and space to have our internal dialogue. You need to find what works for you.

This chapter includes lots of habits from different people at different life stages; habits that help them to reflect on their rational-emotional balance. I hope some of them will spark an idea that helps you.

TAKING TIME...

I enjoy my time by myself going on a walk and praying 3 mornings a week.

I love reading and writing in my journals, I have quite a few different ones for different things! But my favourite time is what I call my creative time. This is time by myself pouring my thoughts or ideas out into one of my little online jotters! This keeps me going most days!

I get up 15 minutes early each morning and spend time reading through the Bible. I use a 'journalling' Bible so I can note down my thoughts.

I am an early riser and tend to spend the first 10-15 minutes of my day in bed just doing some slow breathing and singing in my head. I usually have a tune that comes up one way or the other.

At the beginning of my day, I walk for about half an hour and pray. This is good exercise and an opportunity to review the day to come with God.

We try to apply the Sabbath principle and have a day each week that is for rest and restoration and not filled with jobs and activity.

Each day I carve out some time (sometimes it's only 30 mins, sometimes more) to do an activity that refreshes me. I take a few deep breaths, relax my muscles and read a novel/ bible, a nap, watch something uplifting or do some exercise.

I spend (nearly) every Friday morning at a local prayer house. This is time for me to connect with God away from my house and all its jobs. I can process life here, taking time to notice and work through how I'm feeling. And it's a place of rest, physically and spiritually.

Especially during seasons of high stress, I write in a journal before bed. My journal is completely private to me. I don't try and organise it; I just write down every thought that I can, even the ridiculous ones. I write good and bad things in my journal, just as they occur to me. I often hear from God while I'm writing and note down what he says too. The journalling helps me process things that have happened and get out in a safe way the emotions I'm feeling, which often leads to better sleep.

When I need to process my emotions, I will do something creative. Anything from baking, to gardening, to designing and making clothes, to painting and DIY. I can mull over everything in my head as I dig the garden, sometimes letting out frustrations or anger. I enjoy the slower pace and the chance to breathe.

I go walking in the countryside at least once a week. I allow my mind to wander wherever it wants to but if I find myself thinking about tasks I force myself to ignore the thought. After a while (20+ minutes) I focus on how I am feeling. I reflect on this for a while and then talk to God, explaining how I feel and listening for his input.

BUILDING GOOD BOUNDARIES

I don't look at my phone or computer after 9pm, instead spending time with family and winding down before bed.

I limit evening engagements to 3 per week, so that there are some evenings of rest.

I keep my phone away from me or on silent for much of the day and respond to texts, messages and emails at times during the day when it is convenient to me. This might be frustrating for other people, but I learnt a long time ago it is up to me to look after my mental health and pressure from others, not them!

We try to make sure there are margins in our lives – we don't fill the diary up to capacity, so that there's a buffer if something goes wrong, one of us gets ill, etc.

I compartmentalise a lot of what I do and I prioritise the workload too. Some things are immovable like work but most thing are flexible to a degree. I am just one person and can only go so far even if I think I can meet the greater need.

I'm continuing to learn how to listen to my body and that each day my capacity changes. Instead of ignoring how I feel, I tell myself the jobs can wait for another day, there will always be jobs, so I need to choose rest.

We try to balance our diary carefully. We avoid having more than two busy weekends in a row. This sometimes means saying no to things, but it is much better for our family life than being continually busy!

LIVING WELL

I used to get into infrequent but regular interactions with people that caused me a great deal of emotional stress. God taught me a healthy habit. To firstly recognise it was happening, then ask the Spirit for help in the moment, then gracefully retreat until I had time and space to articulate what I really wanted to say to the person. Now instead of grappling in conflict with these people, I grapple with God in prayer as he shows me my own part in the conflict and helps me behave according to his ways in that situation. When I practice this discipline, the results are way better!

I have two friends I pray with every week. We spend time talking about how we're doing, what's going on in our lives and other things we want to pray about. I've been through some fairly major challenges the last few years and I know one of the main reasons I've been able to maintain a healthy emotional balance is the processing I get to do with these precious friends. I'm an external processor so it really helps to have people to talk to and not just my own thoughts. But then, even better, once we've talked, we take it to God and that's where the healing and perspective-change happens.

With close friends, I deliberately vocalise things as they come up rather than letting them build into something big and complex. Being regularly honest and vulnerable with others actually helps keep me healthy.

Sometimes all I need is a hug or a reassuring presence of someone with me, holding me and that works just fine!

In our family we try to banish the word 'should' from our vocabulary! And to recognise that busyness is not a virtue, and therefore to only say yes to the things we feel God wants us to do not the things that we, or someone else, thinks we should do.

Meeting with my small group each week is a thing that energises me. I come away feeling spiritually, emotionally & often physically lifted and so I make it a priority to be there even if I don't feel like I want to go. I haven't always felt that way about small group meetings, but it seems to be a particular gift from God in a season of low capacity and ill health.

I'm learning to appreciate the benefits of being outdoors for my whole family. Fresh air, physical exercise and an appreciation for the big and small elements of the natural world do us so much good. We're trying to make sure we go for a walk (sometimes really short!) every Saturday and Sunday, especially when we don't feel like it!

It can be extremely difficult when you have young children to carve out time by yourself, let alone have energy to process things! I try to turn to God in prayer or worship whenever I feel overwhelmed. This might be singing a worship song while soothing an unhappy baby – something that helps regulate my emotions and calm them. Sometimes I pray while awake in the middle of the night feeding a child. And when my children are all over the place emotionally, I take a moment to breathe and pray for the patience and insight I need to help them before I get involved. This really helps – I'm demonstrating good emotional control in front of them, and also seeking God for things they may not be able to express!

Printed in Great Britain
by Amazon

58214074R00046